HUNGA
COOKBOOK

Traditional Recipes from Hungary

LIAM LUXE

Copyright © 2023 Liam Luxe

All rights reserved.

CONTENTS

INTRODUCTION i
SOUPS 1
    Goulash Soup 1
    Fisherman's Soup (Halászlé) 2
    Bean and Sausage Soup (Bableves) 3
    Chicken Paprikash Soup 5
    Lentil Soup with Smoked Sausage 6
    Hungarian Mushroom Soup 7
    Tarhonya Soup 8
    Sour Cherry Soup (Hideg Meggyleves) 9
    Potato Leek Soup with Paprika 10
APPETIZERS 12
    Stuffed Peppers (Töltött Paprika) 12
    Hungarian Eggplant Spread (Lecso) 13
    Potato Pancakes (Rántott Krumpli) 14
    Lángos (Fried Bread) 16
    Cheese Pogácsa 17
    Mushroom Pâté 18
    Cabbage Rolls (Töltött Káposzta) 19
    Hungarian Stuffed Mushrooms 21
MAIN DISHES - MEAT 23
    Chicken Paprikash 23
    Beef Goulash 24

Porkolt (Pörkölt) 25
Hungarian Stuffed Peppers (Töltött Paprika) 27
Lamb Stew with Vegetables 28
Chicken and Rice Casserole (Rakott Csirke) 29
Meatballs in Tomato Sauce (Fasírt) 31
MAIN DISHES - POULTRY 33
Hungarian Chicken Schnitzel 33
Turkey Paprikash 34
Duck with Red Cabbage 36
Chicken with Paprika and Dumplings (Csirkepaprikás Nokedlivel) 37
MAIN DISHES - FISH 40
Fish Paprikash 40
Catfish Stew (Harcsapaprikás) 41
Trout with Almonds 43
Crispy Fried Perch (Sült Fogas) 44
SIDE DISHES 46
Nokedli (Hungarian Dumplings) 46
Cucumber Salad (Uborkasaláta) 47
Lecso (Hungarian Eggplant Spread) 48
Stuffed Bell Peppers with Rice (Töltött Paprika Rizzsel) 49
BREADS 51
Hungarian Lángos Bread 51
Walnut Roll (Diós Beigli) 53
Poppy Seed Roll (Mákos Beigli) 55
Hungarian Crescent Rolls (Kifli) 58

Potato Bread (Krumplis Kenyér) 60
VEGETARIAN DELIGHTS 62
Lentil and Vegetable Stew 62
Mushroom Paprikash 63
Eggplant Paprikash 64
Cabbage and Noodles (Kaposztás Tészta) 66
PASTA AND DUMPLINGS 68
Hungarian Noodles with Cabbage (Káposztás Tészta) 68
Cottage Cheese Noodles (Túrós Csusza) 69
Plum Dumplings (Szilvás Gombóc) 70
Cherry Dumplings (Meggyes Gombóc) 73
DESSERTS 76
Dobos Torte 76
Hungarian Apple Strudel (Almás Rétes) 78
Somlói Galuska 80
Rákóczi Túrós 83
Esterházy Torte 85
Chestnut Puree (Gesztenyepüré) 87
Gerbeaud Slice (Zserbó) 89
Rákóczi Túrós 91
MEASUREMENT CONVERSIONS 94

INTRODUCTION

Hungary is a country in Europe, and its food is known for being really tasty and colorful. The recipes here have been enjoyed by Hungarian families for a long time, and now you can make them too.

Easy-to-Follow Recipes

Whether you're someone who loves to cook or you're just starting, these recipes are made to be easy to understand. Each recipe has clear steps to help you enjoy making Hungarian food.

Mixing Old and New

Some recipes are really old and special to Hungary, and are included. But to try new things, you'll find a mix of classic and modern twists on these recipes.

Sharing Food Happiness

Food is like a language that everyone can understand. This cookbook is an invitation to share tasty Hungarian meals with the people you care about. Whether it's a big celebration or just a cozy meal, these recipes are made for sharing good times.

Happy cooking!

SOUPS

GOULASH SOUP

Servings: 6

Time: 1.5 hours

Ingredients:

- 1.5 lbs (700g) beef stew meat, cubed
- 2 onions, finely chopped
- 2 cloves garlic, minced
- 2 tbsp vegetable oil
- 2 tbsp sweet paprika
- 1 tsp caraway seeds
- 1 red bell pepper, diced
- 1 tomato, chopped

- 2 potatoes, peeled and diced
- 4 cups beef broth
- Salt and pepper to taste
- Chopped fresh parsley for garnish

Instructions:

1. In a large pot, heat vegetable oil over medium heat. Add onions and garlic, sauté until softened.
2. Add beef cubes and brown on all sides. Sprinkle paprika over the meat, stirring to coat evenly.
3. Stir in caraway seeds, diced bell pepper, and chopped tomato. Cook for a few minutes until the vegetables begin to soften.
4. Pour in beef broth and add diced potatoes. Bring the soup to a boil, then reduce the heat to low. Simmer for about 1 hour or until the meat is tender.
5. Season with salt and pepper to taste. If you like it spicier, you can add more paprika.
6. Serve hot, garnished with chopped fresh parsley.

FISHERMAN'S SOUP (HALÁSZLÉ)

Servings: 4

Time: 1.5 hours

Ingredients:

- 1 lb (450g) mixed freshwater fish fillets (carp, catfish, perch), cut into chunks
- 1 onion, finely chopped
- 2 cloves garlic, minced

- 2 tbsp vegetable oil
- 2 tbsp sweet paprika
- 1 tsp hot paprika (optional, for heat)
- 1 tomato, chopped
- 1 green bell pepper, diced
- 1.5 quarts (6 cups) fish or vegetable broth
- Salt and pepper to taste
- Fresh lemon wedges for serving
- Chopped fresh parsley for garnish

Instructions:

1. In a large pot, heat vegetable oil over medium heat. Add chopped onions and garlic, sauté until softened.
2. Sprinkle sweet paprika (and hot paprika if desired) over the onions, stirring to coat evenly.
3. Add chopped tomato and diced green bell pepper to the pot. Cook for a few minutes until the vegetables begin to soften.
4. Pour in the fish or vegetable broth and bring it to a simmer.
5. Gently place the fish chunks into the pot. Simmer for about 30-40 minutes until the fish is cooked through and flakes easily.
6. Season with salt and pepper to taste. Adjust the level of spiciness by adding more hot paprika if desired.
7. Serve hot, garnished with chopped fresh parsley and accompanied by lemon wedges.

BEAN AND SAUSAGE SOUP (BABLEVES)

Servings: 6

Time: 1 hour

Ingredients:

- 1 cup dried white beans, soaked overnight
- 1 onion, finely chopped
- 2 carrots, peeled and diced
- 2 cloves garlic, minced
- 2 tbsp vegetable oil
- 1 lb (450g) smoked sausage, sliced
- 1 tsp sweet paprika
- 1 bay leaf
- 6 cups chicken or vegetable broth
- Salt and pepper to taste
- Chopped fresh parsley for garnish

Instructions:

1. In a large pot, heat vegetable oil over medium heat. Add chopped onions, carrots, and garlic. Sauté until the vegetables are softened.
2. Add sliced smoked sausage to the pot. Cook until the sausage is browned and releases its flavor.
3. Sprinkle sweet paprika over the mixture, stirring to coat evenly.
4. Drain the soaked white beans and add them to the pot. Stir to combine.
5. Pour in the chicken or vegetable broth, add a bay leaf, and bring the soup to a simmer.
6. Cover and let it simmer for about 40-50 minutes or until the beans are tender.
7. Season with salt and pepper to taste.
8. Serve hot, garnished with chopped fresh parsley.

CHICKEN PAPRIKASH SOUP

Servings: 4

Time: 45 minutes

Ingredients:

- 1 lb (450g) boneless, skinless chicken thighs, cut into bite-sized pieces
- 1 onion, finely chopped
- 2 cloves garlic, minced
- 2 tbsp vegetable oil
- 2 tbsp sweet paprika
- 1 red bell pepper, diced
- 2 tomatoes, chopped
- 6 cups chicken broth
- 1 cup egg noodles
- Salt and pepper to taste
- Sour cream for garnish
- Chopped fresh parsley for garnish

Instructions:

1. In a large pot, heat vegetable oil over medium heat. Add chopped onions and garlic. Sauté until the onions are translucent.
2. Add chicken pieces to the pot. Brown the chicken on all sides.
3. Sprinkle sweet paprika over the chicken, stirring to coat evenly.
4. Add diced red bell pepper and chopped tomatoes. Cook for a few minutes until the vegetables are softened.

5. Pour in the chicken broth and bring the soup to a boil. Reduce the heat to low and let it simmer for 20 minutes.
6. Add egg noodles to the pot and cook until they are tender.
7. Season with salt and pepper to taste.
8. Serve hot, garnished with a dollop of sour cream and chopped fresh parsley.

LENTIL SOUP WITH SMOKED SAUSAGE

Servings: 6

Time: 1 hour

Ingredients:

- 1 cup dried green lentils, rinsed
- 1 onion, finely chopped
- 2 carrots, peeled and diced
- 2 cloves garlic, minced
- 2 tbsp vegetable oil
- 1 lb (450g) smoked sausage, sliced
- 1 tsp dried thyme
- 1 bay leaf
- 6 cups chicken or vegetable broth
- Salt and pepper to taste
- Fresh lemon wedges for serving
- Chopped fresh parsley for garnish

Instructions:

1. In a large pot, heat vegetable oil over medium heat. Add chopped onions, carrots, and garlic. Sauté until the vegetables are softened.
2. Add sliced smoked sausage to the pot. Cook until the sausage is browned and imparts its smoky flavor.
3. Stir in dried green lentils, thyme, and bay leaf.
4. Pour in the chicken or vegetable broth and bring the soup to a simmer.
5. Cover and let it simmer for about 40-45 minutes or until the lentils are tender.
6. Season with salt and pepper to taste.
7. Serve hot, garnished with fresh lemon wedges and chopped parsley.

HUNGARIAN MUSHROOM SOUP

Servings: 4

Time: 40 minutes

Ingredients:

- 1 lb (450g) mushrooms, sliced
- 1 onion, finely chopped
- 2 cloves garlic, minced
- 2 tbsp butter
- 2 tbsp all-purpose flour
- 4 cups vegetable broth
- 1 tsp dried dill
- 1 tsp sweet paprika
- 1 cup milk
- Salt and pepper to taste
- Sour cream for garnish

- Chopped fresh parsley for garnish

Instructions:

1. In a large pot, melt butter over medium heat. Add chopped onions and garlic. Sauté until the onions are translucent.
2. Add sliced mushrooms to the pot. Cook until the mushrooms release their moisture and become golden brown.
3. Sprinkle flour over the mushrooms, stirring to create a roux.
4. Pour in the vegetable broth, stirring continuously to avoid lumps.
5. Add dried dill and sweet paprika to the pot. Let it simmer for 15-20 minutes.
6. Stir in the milk and continue simmering until the soup is heated through.
7. Season with salt and pepper to taste.
8. Serve hot, garnished with a dollop of sour cream and chopped fresh parsley.

TARHONYA SOUP

Servings: 4

Time: 30 minutes

Ingredients:

- 1 cup tarhonya (Hungarian egg pasta)
- 1 onion, finely chopped
- 2 carrots, peeled and diced

- 2 cloves garlic, minced
- 2 tbsp vegetable oil
- 4 cups chicken or vegetable broth
- 1 tsp dried thyme
- Salt and pepper to taste
- Chopped fresh parsley for garnish

Instructions:

1. In a medium-sized pot, heat vegetable oil over medium heat. Add chopped onions, carrots, and garlic. Sauté until the vegetables are softened.
2. Add tarhonya to the pot and cook until it turns golden brown, stirring frequently.
3. Pour in the chicken or vegetable broth and add dried thyme.
4. Bring the soup to a simmer and let it cook for about 15-20 minutes or until the tarhonya is tender.
5. Season with salt and pepper to taste.
6. Serve hot, garnished with chopped fresh parsley.

SOUR CHERRY SOUP (HIDEG MEGGYLEVES)

Servings: 4

Time: 30 minutes (plus chilling time)

Ingredients:

- 2 cups pitted sour cherries (fresh or canned)
- 1 cup cherry juice
- 1/2 cup sugar

- 1 cinnamon stick
- 1 lemon, zest and juice
- 2 cups water
- 2 tbsp cornstarch
- 1 cup sour cream
- Mint leaves for garnish

Instructions:

1. In a pot, combine pitted sour cherries, cherry juice, sugar, cinnamon stick, lemon zest, and water. Bring it to a boil, then reduce the heat and simmer for 10-15 minutes.
2. In a small bowl, mix cornstarch with a little water to create a slurry. Stir the slurry into the soup to thicken it slightly.
3. Remove the soup from heat and let it cool to room temperature.
4. Once cooled, stir in the lemon juice and refrigerate the soup for at least 2 hours or until chilled.
5. Before serving, remove the cinnamon stick.
6. To serve, ladle the chilled soup into bowls and swirl in a spoonful of sour cream.
7. Garnish with fresh mint leaves.
8. Enjoy the refreshing and sweet-tart flavors of Sour Cherry Soup, a delightful Hungarian summer treat!

POTATO LEEK SOUP WITH PAPRIKA

Servings: 6

Time: 45 minutes

Ingredients:

- 3 leeks, white and light green parts, sliced
- 4 potatoes, peeled and diced
- 2 tbsp butter
- 1 onion, chopped
- 2 cloves garlic, minced
- 1 tsp sweet paprika
- 6 cups vegetable broth
- Salt and pepper to taste
- 1 cup milk
- Chopped fresh chives for garnish

Instructions:

1. In a large pot, melt butter over medium heat. Add chopped onions, leeks, and garlic. Sauté until they are softened.
2. Sprinkle sweet paprika over the vegetables, stirring to coat evenly.
3. Add diced potatoes to the pot. Cook for a few minutes to combine the flavors.
4. Pour in the vegetable broth and bring the soup to a boil. Reduce the heat to low, cover, and simmer for about 20-25 minutes or until the potatoes are tender.
5. Season with salt and pepper to taste.
6. Using an immersion blender, blend the soup until smooth. Alternatively, transfer the soup to a blender in batches.
7. Stir in the milk and let the soup simmer for an additional 5 minutes.
8. Serve hot, garnished with chopped fresh chives.

APPETIZERS

STUFFED PEPPERS (TÖLTÖTT PAPRIKA)

Servings: 4

Time: 1.5 hours

Ingredients:

- 4 large bell peppers, halved and seeds removed
- 1 lb (450g) ground pork or beef
- 1 cup rice, cooked
- 1 onion, finely chopped
- 2 cloves garlic, minced
- 2 tbsp vegetable oil
- 2 tbsp sweet paprika
- 1 tsp caraway seeds

- 1 cup tomato sauce
- Salt and pepper to taste
- Sour cream for serving
- Chopped fresh parsley for garnish

Instructions:

1. Preheat the oven to 375°F (190°C).
2. In a skillet, heat vegetable oil over medium heat. Add chopped onions and garlic. Sauté until the onions are translucent.
3. Add ground meat to the skillet. Cook until browned, breaking it apart with a spoon.
4. Stir in cooked rice, sweet paprika, caraway seeds, salt, and pepper. Cook for a few minutes to blend the flavors.
5. Fill each bell pepper half with the meat and rice mixture.
6. Place the stuffed peppers in a baking dish. Pour tomato sauce over the peppers.
7. Cover the baking dish with aluminum foil and bake for 45-50 minutes or until the peppers are tender.
8. Serve hot, topped with a dollop of sour cream and garnished with chopped fresh parsley.

HUNGARIAN EGGPLANT SPREAD (LECSO)

Servings: 6

Time: 45 minutes

Ingredients:

- 2 large eggplants, diced

- 2 bell peppers, diced
- 2 tomatoes, diced
- 1 onion, finely chopped
- 2 cloves garlic, minced
- 3 tbsp vegetable oil
- 2 tsp sweet paprika
- Salt and pepper to taste
- Fresh parsley for garnish

Instructions:

1. In a large skillet, heat vegetable oil over medium heat. Add chopped onions and garlic. Sauté until the onions are translucent.
2. Add diced eggplants, bell peppers, and tomatoes to the skillet. Cook until the vegetables are soft and the liquids release.
3. Sprinkle sweet paprika over the vegetables, stirring to coat evenly.
4. Reduce the heat to low, cover the skillet, and let the mixture simmer for about 30 minutes, stirring occasionally.
5. Season with salt and pepper to taste.
6. Using a fork or potato masher, mash the vegetables to achieve a spreadable consistency.
7. Let the spread cool to room temperature.
8. Serve chilled or at room temperature, garnished with fresh parsley.

POTATO PANCAKES (RÁNTOTT KRUMPLI)

Servings: 4

Time: 30 minutes

Ingredients:

- 4 large potatoes, peeled and grated
- 1 onion, finely chopped
- 2 eggs
- 3 tbsp all-purpose flour
- 1 tsp salt
- 1/2 tsp black pepper
- Vegetable oil for frying
- Sour cream for serving
- Applesauce for serving (optional)

Instructions:

1. Grate the peeled potatoes using a box grater. Squeeze out excess liquid using a clean kitchen towel.
2. In a bowl, combine grated potatoes, chopped onions, eggs, flour, salt, and black pepper. Mix well until a batter forms.
3. In a large skillet, heat vegetable oil over medium-high heat.
4. Drop spoonfuls of the potato batter into the hot oil, flattening them with the back of the spoon to form pancakes.
5. Fry the pancakes for about 3-4 minutes on each side or until they are golden brown and crispy.
6. Remove the pancakes from the skillet and place them on a plate lined with paper towels to absorb excess oil.

7. Serve hot, accompanied by a dollop of sour cream. For a sweet twist, try them with applesauce on the side.

LÁNGOS (FRIED BREAD)

Servings: 6

Time: 1 hour (including dough rising time)

Ingredients:

- 3 cups all-purpose flour
- 1 cup warm milk
- 1 tsp sugar
- 1 tsp salt
- 2 tsp active dry yeast
- Vegetable oil for frying
- Garlic, minced (optional, for topping)
- Sour cream (optional, for topping)
- Grated cheese (optional, for topping)

Instructions:

1. In a small bowl, combine warm milk and sugar. Sprinkle yeast over the mixture and let it sit for about 5-10 minutes until it becomes frothy.
2. In a large bowl, combine flour and salt. Make a well in the center and pour in the yeast mixture.
3. Mix the ingredients to form a dough. Knead the dough on a floured surface for about 5-7 minutes until it becomes smooth.

4. Place the dough in a lightly oiled bowl, cover it with a clean kitchen towel, and let it rise in a warm place for about 30 minutes or until it doubles in size.
5. Punch down the risen dough and divide it into small portions. Roll each portion into a ball.
6. Flatten each ball into a disk, making sure it's not too thin.
7. In a deep pan, heat vegetable oil to 350°F (175°C). Carefully place each dough disk into the hot oil and fry until both sides are golden brown.
8. Remove the fried bread from the oil and place it on paper towels to absorb excess oil.
9. Optionally, top each Lángos with minced garlic, sour cream, and grated cheese.
10. Serve hot.

CHEESE POGÁCSA

Servings: 24

Time: 45 minutes

Ingredients:

- 3 cups all-purpose flour
- 1 cup unsalted butter, softened
- 1 cup grated cheese (cheddar or Gouda)
- 2 tsp baking powder
- 1/2 tsp salt
- 2 eggs
- 1/2 cup sour cream
- 1/4 cup milk
- 1 egg yolk (for egg wash)
- Sesame seeds or poppy seeds for topping

Instructions:

1. Preheat the oven to 375°F (190°C). Line a baking sheet with parchment paper.
2. In a large bowl, combine flour, baking powder, and salt.
3. Add softened butter to the flour mixture and mix until it resembles coarse crumbs.
4. Stir in grated cheese.
5. In a separate bowl, whisk together eggs, sour cream, and milk.
6. Add the wet ingredients to the flour mixture. Mix until a soft dough forms.
7. On a floured surface, roll out the dough to about 1/2-inch thickness.
8. Using a round cookie cutter, cut out circles and place them on the prepared baking sheet.
9. In a small bowl, beat the egg yolk with a little water. Brush the tops of the pogácsa with the egg wash.
10. Sprinkle sesame seeds or poppy seeds on top of each pogácsa.
11. Bake for 15-18 minutes or until the tops are golden brown.
12. Allow the cheese pogácsa to cool slightly before serving.

MUSHROOM PÂTÉ

Servings: 8

Time: 30 minutes

Ingredients:

- 1 lb (450g) mushrooms, finely chopped

- 1 onion, finely chopped
- 2 cloves garlic, minced
- 2 tbsp butter
- 1/4 cup cream cheese
- 1/4 cup sour cream
- 2 tbsp chopped fresh parsley
- Salt and pepper to taste
- Toasted baguette slices or crackers for serving

Instructions:

1. In a skillet, melt butter over medium heat. Add chopped onions and garlic. Sauté until the onions are translucent.
2. Add finely chopped mushrooms to the skillet. Cook until the mushrooms release their moisture and become golden brown.
3. Reduce the heat to low. Stir in cream cheese and sour cream until well combined.
4. Cook the mixture for an additional 5-7 minutes, allowing it to thicken.
5. Remove the skillet from heat and let the mixture cool slightly.
6. Transfer the mushroom mixture to a food processor. Add chopped fresh parsley, salt, and pepper.
7. Pulse the ingredients until you achieve a smooth consistency.
8. Taste and adjust the seasoning if needed.
9. Transfer the mushroom pâté to a serving bowl.
10. Serve at room temperature with toasted baguette slices or crackers.

CABBAGE ROLLS (TÖLTÖTT KÁPOSZTA)

Servings: 6

Time: 2 hours

Ingredients:

- 1 large head of cabbage
- 1 lb (450g) ground pork
- 1 cup rice, cooked
- 1 onion, finely chopped
- 2 cloves garlic, minced
- 2 tbsp vegetable oil
- 2 tbsp sweet paprika
- 1 tsp caraway seeds
- 1 can (14 oz) crushed tomatoes
- 2 cups beef broth
- Salt and pepper to taste
- Sour cream for serving
- Chopped fresh parsley for garnish

Instructions:

1. Preheat the oven to 350°F (175°C).
2. Bring a large pot of water to a boil. Carefully place the whole head of cabbage into the boiling water. Cook for about 5-7 minutes, or until the outer leaves are tender and pliable.
3. Remove the cabbage from the water and carefully peel off the softened leaves. Set them aside.
4. In a skillet, heat vegetable oil over medium heat. Add chopped onions and garlic. Sauté until the onions are translucent.

5. Add ground pork to the skillet. Cook until browned, breaking it apart with a spoon.
6. Stir in cooked rice, sweet paprika, caraway seeds, salt, and pepper. Cook for a few minutes to blend the flavors.
7. Place a spoonful of the pork and rice mixture onto each cabbage leaf. Roll the leaves, folding the sides inward, to form cabbage rolls.
8. Place the cabbage rolls seam-side down in a baking dish.
9. In a bowl, mix crushed tomatoes and beef broth. Pour the mixture over the cabbage rolls.
10. Cover the baking dish with aluminum foil and bake for 1.5 hours, or until the cabbage is tender.
11. Serve hot, topped with a dollop of sour cream and garnished with chopped fresh parsley.

HUNGARIAN STUFFED MUSHROOMS

Servings: 12

Time: 40 minutes

Ingredients:

- 24 large mushrooms, stems removed and finely chopped
- 1/2 lb (225g) ground pork or sausage
- 1 onion, finely chopped
- 2 cloves garlic, minced
- 2 tbsp vegetable oil
- 2 tbsp breadcrumbs
- 1/4 cup sour cream
- 1 tsp sweet paprika
- Salt and pepper to taste
- Fresh parsley for garnish

Instructions:

1. Preheat the oven to 375°F (190°C).
2. Clean the mushrooms and remove the stems. Finely chop the mushroom stems.
3. In a skillet, heat vegetable oil over medium heat. Add chopped onions and garlic. Sauté until the onions are translucent.
4. Add ground pork or sausage to the skillet. Cook until browned, breaking it apart with a spoon.
5. Stir in chopped mushroom stems and cook until the liquid evaporates.
6. Remove the skillet from heat and let it cool slightly.
7. In a bowl, combine the cooked pork mixture with breadcrumbs, sour cream, sweet paprika, salt, and pepper. Mix well.
8. Fill each mushroom cap with the pork mixture.
9. Place the stuffed mushrooms on a baking sheet.
10. Bake for 20-25 minutes or until the mushrooms are tender and the filling is golden brown.
11. Garnish with fresh parsley and serve hot.

MAIN DISHES - MEAT

CHICKEN PAPRIKASH

Servings: 4

Time: 1.5 hours

Ingredients:

- 1 whole chicken, cut into parts
- 2 tbsp vegetable oil
- 2 onions, finely chopped
- 2 cloves garlic, minced
- 2 tbsp sweet paprika
- 1 tomato, chopped
- 1 green bell pepper, sliced
- 1 cup chicken broth

- 1 cup sour cream
- Salt and pepper to taste
- Chopped fresh parsley for garnish
- Egg noodles or rice for serving

Instructions:

1. In a large pot, heat vegetable oil over medium heat. Brown the chicken pieces on all sides. Remove the chicken and set it aside.
2. In the same pot, add chopped onions and garlic. Sauté until the onions are translucent.
3. Stir in sweet paprika, coating the onions and garlic evenly.
4. Add chopped tomatoes and sliced green bell peppers. Cook until the vegetables are softened.
5. Return the browned chicken to the pot. Pour in chicken broth, ensuring the chicken is partially submerged. Bring it to a simmer.
6. Cover the pot and let it simmer for about 45 minutes to 1 hour or until the chicken is cooked through and tender.
7. In a bowl, mix sour cream with a ladle of hot broth from the pot to temper it. Gradually add the sour cream mixture back to the pot, stirring continuously.
8. Season with salt and pepper to taste. Let it simmer for an additional 10 minutes.
9. Serve the Chicken Paprikash over egg noodles or rice, garnished with chopped fresh parsley.

BEEF GOULASH

Servings: 6

Time: 2 hours

Ingredients:

- 2 lbs (900g) beef stew meat, cubed
- 2 onions, finely chopped
- 3 cloves garlic, minced
- 3 tbsp vegetable oil
- 3 tbsp sweet paprika
- 1 tbsp caraway seeds
- 1 can (14 oz) crushed tomatoes
- 3 cups beef broth
- 2 bay leaves
- Salt and pepper to taste
- 3 large potatoes, peeled and diced
- Chopped fresh parsley for garnish

Instructions:

1. In a large pot, heat vegetable oil over medium heat. Add chopped onions and garlic. Sauté until the onions are translucent.
2. Add cubed beef to the pot. Brown the meat on all sides.
3. Sprinkle sweet paprika and caraway seeds over the meat, stirring to coat evenly.
4. Pour in crushed tomatoes and beef broth. Add bay leaves and season with salt and pepper. Bring it to a boil.
5. Reduce the heat to low, cover the pot, and let it simmer for 1.5 hours or until the beef is tender.
6. Add diced potatoes to the pot. Simmer for an additional 30 minutes or until the potatoes are cooked through.
7. Adjust the seasoning if needed and remove the bay leaves.

8. Serve hot, garnished with chopped fresh parsley.

PORKOLT (PÖRKÖLT)

Servings: 4

Time: 1.5 hours

Ingredients:

- 2 lbs (900g) pork shoulder, cut into cubes
- 2 onions, finely chopped
- 3 cloves garlic, minced
- 3 tbsp vegetable oil
- 2 tbsp sweet paprika
- 1 tsp caraway seeds
- 2 tomatoes, chopped
- 1 red bell pepper, sliced
- 1 green bell pepper, sliced
- 1 cup beef broth
- Salt and pepper to taste
- Chopped fresh parsley for garnish
- Egg noodles or rice for serving

Instructions:

1. In a large pot, heat vegetable oil over medium heat. Add chopped onions and garlic. Sauté until the onions are translucent.
2. Add cubed pork to the pot. Brown the pork on all sides.
3. Sprinkle sweet paprika and caraway seeds over the pork, stirring to coat evenly.

4. Add chopped tomatoes and sliced bell peppers to the pot. Cook for a few minutes until the vegetables are softened.
5. Pour in beef broth, season with salt and pepper, and bring it to a simmer.
6. Cover the pot and let it simmer for 1.5 hours or until the pork is tender.
7. Adjust the seasoning if needed.
8. Serve the Porkolt over egg noodles or rice, garnished with chopped fresh parsley.

HUNGARIAN STUFFED PEPPERS (TÖLTÖTT PAPRIKA)

Servings: 4

Time: 1.5 hours

Ingredients:

- 4 large bell peppers, halved and seeds removed
- 1 lb (450g) ground pork or beef
- 1 cup rice, cooked
- 1 onion, finely chopped
- 2 cloves garlic, minced
- 2 tbsp vegetable oil
- 2 tbsp sweet paprika
- 1 tsp caraway seeds
- 1 cup tomato sauce
- Salt and pepper to taste
- Sour cream for serving
- Chopped fresh parsley for garnish

Instructions:

1. Preheat the oven to 375°F (190°C).
2. In a skillet, heat vegetable oil over medium heat. Add chopped onions and garlic. Sauté until the onions are translucent.
3. Add ground pork or beef to the skillet. Cook until browned, breaking it apart with a spoon.
4. Stir in cooked rice, sweet paprika, caraway seeds, salt, and pepper. Cook for a few minutes to blend the flavors.
5. Fill each bell pepper half with the meat and rice mixture.
6. Place the stuffed peppers in a baking dish. Pour tomato sauce over the peppers.
7. Cover the baking dish with aluminum foil and bake for 45-50 minutes or until the peppers are tender.
8. Serve hot, topped with a dollop of sour cream and garnished with chopped fresh parsley.

LAMB STEW WITH VEGETABLES

Servings: 6

Time: 2.5 hours

Ingredients:

- 2 lbs (900g) lamb shoulder, cut into cubes
- 2 onions, finely chopped
- 3 cloves garlic, minced
- 3 tbsp vegetable oil
- 2 tbsp sweet paprika
- 1 tsp caraway seeds
- 3 carrots, peeled and sliced

- 3 potatoes, peeled and diced
- 1 parsnip, peeled and diced
- 2 cups beef or vegetable broth
- 1 cup red wine
- Salt and pepper to taste
- Chopped fresh parsley for garnish

Instructions:

1. In a large pot, heat vegetable oil over medium heat. Add chopped onions and garlic. Sauté until the onions are translucent.
2. Add cubed lamb to the pot. Brown the lamb on all sides.
3. Sprinkle sweet paprika and caraway seeds over the lamb, stirring to coat evenly.
4. Pour in beef or vegetable broth and red wine. Bring it to a simmer.
5. Cover the pot and let it simmer for 1.5 to 2 hours or until the lamb is tender.
6. Add sliced carrots, diced potatoes, and diced parsnip to the pot. Simmer for an additional 30 minutes or until the vegetables are cooked through.
7. Season with salt and pepper to taste.
8. Serve hot, garnished with chopped fresh parsley.

CHICKEN AND RICE CASSEROLE (RAKOTT CSIRKE)

Servings: 6

Time: 2 hours

Ingredients:

- 1 whole chicken, cut into parts
- 2 cups rice, cooked
- 2 onions, finely chopped
- 3 cloves garlic, minced
- 3 tbsp vegetable oil
- 2 tbsp sweet paprika
- 1 tsp caraway seeds
- 1 cup sour cream
- 1 cup chicken broth
- Salt and pepper to taste
- Butter for greasing the baking dish
- Chopped fresh parsley for garnish

Instructions:

1. Preheat the oven to 375°F (190°C). Grease a large baking dish with butter.
2. In a skillet, heat vegetable oil over medium heat. Add chopped onions and garlic. Sauté until the onions are translucent.
3. Add chicken parts to the skillet. Brown the chicken on all sides.
4. Sprinkle sweet paprika and caraway seeds over the chicken, stirring to coat evenly.
5. In a bowl, mix sour cream with chicken broth.
6. Place a layer of cooked rice in the bottom of the greased baking dish.
7. Arrange the browned chicken on top of the rice.
8. Pour half of the sour cream and chicken broth mixture over the chicken.
9. Add another layer of rice and pour the remaining sour cream and chicken broth mixture.

10. Cover the baking dish with aluminum foil and bake for 1.5 hours or until the chicken is cooked through.
11. Remove the foil and bake for an additional 15-20 minutes or until the top is golden brown.
12. Season with salt and pepper to taste.
13. Serve hot, garnished with chopped fresh parsley.

MEATBALLS IN TOMATO SAUCE (FASÍRT)

Servings: 4

Time: 1 hour

Ingredients:

For the Meatballs:

- 1 lb (450g) ground beef or pork (or a mixture of both)
- 1 onion, finely chopped
- 2 cloves garlic, minced
- 1/2 cup breadcrumbs
- 2 eggs
- Salt and pepper to taste
- Vegetable oil for frying

For the Tomato Sauce:

- 1 can (14 oz) crushed tomatoes
- 1 onion, finely chopped
- 2 cloves garlic, minced
- 2 tbsp vegetable oil
- 1 tsp sweet paprika
- 1 tsp dried oregano

- Salt and pepper to taste
- Chopped fresh parsley for garnish

Instructions:

For the Meatballs:

1. In a bowl, combine ground meat, chopped onions, minced garlic, breadcrumbs, eggs, salt, and pepper. Mix well until all ingredients are evenly incorporated.
2. Form the mixture into meatballs, about 1.5 inches in diameter.
3. In a skillet, heat vegetable oil over medium-high heat. Fry the meatballs until browned on all sides and cooked through. Remove them from the skillet and set aside.

For the Tomato Sauce:

1. In the same skillet, heat vegetable oil over medium heat. Add chopped onions and garlic. Sauté until the onions are translucent.
2. Stir in sweet paprika and dried oregano, coating the onions and garlic evenly.
3. Pour in crushed tomatoes and season with salt and pepper. Bring the sauce to a simmer.
4. Add the fried meatballs to the tomato sauce. Let them simmer in the sauce for about 15-20 minutes.
5. Adjust the seasoning if needed.
6. Serve hot, garnished with chopped fresh parsley.

MAIN DISHES - POULTRY

HUNGARIAN CHICKEN SCHNITZEL

Servings: 4

Time: 30 minutes

Ingredients:

- 4 boneless, skinless chicken breasts
- Salt and pepper to taste
- 1 cup all-purpose flour
- 2 eggs, beaten
- 2 cups breadcrumbs
- Vegetable oil for frying
- Lemon wedges for serving
- Chopped fresh parsley for garnish

Instructions:

1. Place each chicken breast between plastic wrap and pound them with a meat mallet until they are about 1/4 inch thick. Season each piece with salt and pepper.
2. Set up a breading station with three shallow bowls: one with flour, one with beaten eggs, and one with breadcrumbs.
3. Dredge each chicken breast in flour, coating both sides and shaking off excess.
4. Dip the floured chicken in the beaten eggs, ensuring it is well-coated.
5. Press the chicken into the breadcrumbs, making sure it is evenly coated.
6. In a large skillet, heat vegetable oil over medium-high heat.
7. Fry the breaded chicken breasts for about 3-4 minutes per side or until they are golden brown and cooked through.
8. Place the schnitzels on a paper towel-lined plate to absorb excess oil.
9. Garnish with chopped fresh parsley and serve hot with lemon wedges on the side.

TURKEY PAPRIKASH

Servings: 4

Time: 1.5 hours

Ingredients:

- 1 lb (450g) turkey breast, cut into cubes
- 2 onions, finely chopped

- 2 cloves garlic, minced
- 3 tbsp vegetable oil
- 2 tbsp sweet paprika
- 1 tomato, chopped
- 1 green bell pepper, sliced
- 1 cup chicken broth
- 1 cup sour cream
- Salt and pepper to taste
- Chopped fresh parsley for garnish
- Egg noodles or rice for serving

Instructions:

1. In a large pot, heat vegetable oil over medium heat. Add chopped onions and garlic. Sauté until the onions are translucent.
2. Add cubed turkey to the pot. Brown the turkey on all sides.
3. Sprinkle sweet paprika over the turkey, stirring to coat evenly.
4. Add chopped tomatoes and sliced green bell peppers to the pot. Cook for a few minutes until the vegetables are softened.
5. Pour in chicken broth and bring it to a simmer.
6. Cover the pot and let it simmer for 1 hour or until the turkey is tender.
7. In a bowl, mix sour cream with a ladle of hot broth from the pot to temper it. Gradually add the sour cream mixture back to the pot, stirring continuously.
8. Season with salt and pepper to taste. Let it simmer for an additional 15 minutes.
9. Serve the Turkey Paprikash over egg noodles or rice, garnished with chopped fresh parsley.

DUCK WITH RED CABBAGE

Servings: 4

Time: 2.5 hours

Ingredients:

For the Duck:

- 2 duck legs
- Salt and pepper to taste
- 2 tbsp vegetable oil
- 1 onion, finely chopped
- 2 cloves garlic, minced
- 2 cups chicken or duck broth
- 1 cup red wine
- 2 tbsp red currant jelly (optional)
- Chopped fresh thyme for garnish

For the Red Cabbage:

- 1 small red cabbage, shredded
- 2 apples, peeled and diced
- 1 onion, thinly sliced
- 3 tbsp red wine vinegar
- 2 tbsp brown sugar
- 2 tbsp butter
- Salt and pepper to taste

Instructions:

For the Duck:

1. Preheat the oven to 325°F (163°C).
2. Season the duck legs with salt and pepper.
3. In a large oven-safe skillet, heat vegetable oil over medium-high heat. Brown the duck legs on all sides.
4. Remove excess fat from the skillet, leaving about 2 tablespoons.
5. Add chopped onions and garlic to the skillet. Sauté until the onions are translucent.
6. Pour in chicken or duck broth, red wine, and red currant jelly. Bring it to a simmer.
7. Cover the skillet with a lid or foil and transfer it to the preheated oven. Roast for 2 hours or until the duck is tender.
8. Baste the duck with the cooking liquid occasionally.
9. Garnish with chopped fresh thyme before serving.

For the Red Cabbage:

1. In a separate pan, melt butter over medium heat. Add sliced onions and cook until they are soft.
2. Add shredded red cabbage and diced apples to the pan. Sauté for a few minutes.
3. Stir in red wine vinegar and brown sugar. Season with salt and pepper.
4. Cover the pan and let the red cabbage mixture simmer for about 30-40 minutes, stirring occasionally.
5. Adjust the seasoning if needed.
6. Serve the roasted duck legs on a bed of red cabbage.

CHICKEN WITH PAPRIKA AND DUMPLINGS (CSIRKEPAPRIKÁS NOKEDLIVEL)

Servings: 4

Time: 1.5 hours

Ingredients:

For the Chicken:

- 1 whole chicken, cut into parts
- Salt and pepper to taste
- 3 tbsp vegetable oil
- 2 onions, finely chopped
- 2 cloves garlic, minced
- 2 tbsp sweet paprika
- 1 tomato, chopped
- 1 green bell pepper, sliced
- 2 cups chicken broth
- 1 cup sour cream
- Chopped fresh parsley for garnish

For the Dumplings (Nokedli):

- 2 cups all-purpose flour
- 2 eggs
- 1/2 cup milk
- Salt to taste

Instructions:

For the Chicken:

1. Season the chicken parts with salt and pepper.
2. In a large pot, heat vegetable oil over medium-high heat. Brown the chicken on all sides.

3. Remove excess fat from the pot, leaving about 2 tablespoons.
4. Add chopped onions and garlic to the pot. Sauté until the onions are translucent.
5. Stir in sweet paprika, coating the onions and garlic evenly.
6. Add chopped tomatoes and sliced green bell peppers to the pot. Cook for a few minutes until the vegetables are softened.
7. Pour in chicken broth and bring it to a simmer.
8. Cover the pot and let it simmer for 1 hour or until the chicken is cooked through.
9. In a bowl, mix sour cream with a ladle of hot broth from the pot to temper it. Gradually add the sour cream mixture back to the pot, stirring continuously.
10. Season with salt and pepper to taste. Let it simmer for an additional 15 minutes.
11. Garnish with chopped fresh parsley.

For the Dumplings (Nokedli):

1. In a bowl, whisk together eggs, milk, and a pinch of salt.
2. Gradually add flour to the egg mixture, stirring continuously, until a thick batter forms.
3. In a large pot of boiling salted water, spoon small portions of the batter into the water. Cook until the dumplings float to the surface.
4. Remove the dumplings with a slotted spoon and drain.
5. Serve the Chicken with Paprika over the dumplings.

MAIN DISHES - FISH

FISH PAPRIKASH

Servings: 4

Time: 1 hour

Ingredients:

- 4 fish fillets (catfish, carp, or other freshwater fish)
- Salt and pepper to taste
- 3 tbsp vegetable oil
- 2 onions, finely chopped
- 2 cloves garlic, minced
- 2 tbsp sweet paprika
- 1 tomato, chopped
- 1 green bell pepper, sliced

- 2 cups fish or vegetable broth
- 1 cup sour cream
- Chopped fresh parsley for garnish
- Cooked rice or pasta for serving

Instructions:

1. Season the fish fillets with salt and pepper.
2. In a large skillet, heat vegetable oil over medium-high heat. Sear the fish fillets on both sides until golden brown. Remove them from the skillet and set aside.
3. In the same skillet, add chopped onions and garlic. Sauté until the onions are translucent.
4. Stir in sweet paprika, coating the onions and garlic evenly.
5. Add chopped tomatoes and sliced green bell peppers to the skillet. Cook for a few minutes until the vegetables are softened.
6. Pour in fish or vegetable broth and bring it to a simmer.
7. Carefully place the seared fish fillets back into the skillet.
8. Cover the skillet and let it simmer for 15-20 minutes or until the fish is cooked through.
9. In a bowl, mix sour cream with a ladle of hot broth from the skillet to temper it. Gradually add the sour cream mixture back to the skillet, stirring continuously.
10. Season with salt and pepper to taste. Let it simmer for an additional 5-10 minutes.
11. Serve the Fish Paprikash over cooked rice or pasta.
12. Garnish with chopped fresh parsley.

CATFISH STEW (HARCSAPAPRIKÁS)

Servings: 4

Time: 1.5 hours

Ingredients:

- 2 lbs (900g) catfish fillets
- Salt and pepper to taste
- 3 tbsp vegetable oil
- 2 onions, finely chopped
- 2 cloves garlic, minced
- 2 tbsp sweet paprika
- 1 tomato, chopped
- 1 green bell pepper, sliced
- 1 cup fish or vegetable broth
- 1 cup sour cream
- Chopped fresh dill for garnish
- Lemon wedges for serving
- Cooked rice or potatoes for serving

Instructions:

1. Season the catfish fillets with salt and pepper.
2. In a large skillet, heat vegetable oil over medium-high heat. Sear the catfish fillets on both sides until golden brown. Remove them from the skillet and set aside.
3. In the same skillet, add chopped onions and garlic. Sauté until the onions are translucent.
4. Stir in sweet paprika, coating the onions and garlic evenly.
5. Add chopped tomatoes and sliced green bell peppers to the skillet. Cook for a few minutes until the vegetables are softened.
6. Pour in fish or vegetable broth and bring it to a simmer.

7. Carefully place the seared catfish fillets back into the skillet.
8. Cover the skillet and let it simmer for 45-60 minutes or until the fish is cooked through.
9. In a bowl, mix sour cream with a ladle of hot broth from the skillet to temper it. Gradually add the sour cream mixture back to the skillet, stirring continuously.
10. Season with salt and pepper to taste. Let it simmer for an additional 10-15 minutes.
11. Serve the Catfish Stew over cooked rice or potatoes.
12. Garnish with chopped fresh dill and serve with lemon wedges.

TROUT WITH ALMONDS

Servings: 4

Time: 30 minutes

Ingredients:

- 4 trout fillets
- Salt and pepper to taste
- 1/2 cup all-purpose flour
- 3 tbsp vegetable oil
- 1/2 cup sliced almonds
- 2 tbsp butter
- Juice of 1 lemon
- Chopped fresh parsley for garnish
- Lemon wedges for serving
- Cooked rice or potatoes for serving

Instructions:

1. Season the trout fillets with salt and pepper.
2. Dredge each fillet in flour, shaking off any excess.
3. In a large skillet, heat vegetable oil over medium-high heat. Sear the trout fillets on both sides until golden brown. Remove them from the skillet and set aside.
4. In the same skillet, add sliced almonds and butter. Toast the almonds until they are golden and fragrant.
5. Place the seared trout fillets back into the skillet with the almonds.
6. Squeeze the lemon juice over the fillets.
7. Cook for an additional 5-7 minutes, basting the trout with the almond and butter mixture.
8. Season with additional salt and pepper if needed.
9. Serve the Trout with Almonds over cooked rice or potatoes.
10. Garnish with chopped fresh parsley and serve with lemon wedges.

CRISPY FRIED PERCH (SÜLT FOGAS)

Servings: 4

Time: 30 minutes

Ingredients:

- 4 perch fillets
- Salt and pepper to taste
- 1 cup all-purpose flour
- 2 eggs, beaten
- 1 cup breadcrumbs
- 1/2 cup vegetable oil
- Lemon wedges for serving

- Chopped fresh parsley for garnish
- Tartar sauce for dipping (optional)

Instructions:

1. Season the perch fillets with salt and pepper.
2. Dredge each fillet in flour, shaking off any excess.
3. Dip the floured fillets into the beaten eggs, ensuring they are well-coated.
4. Press the fillets into the breadcrumbs, making sure they are evenly coated.
5. In a large skillet, heat vegetable oil over medium-high heat.
6. Fry the breaded perch fillets for 3-4 minutes per side or until they are golden brown and crispy.
7. Remove the fillets from the skillet and place them on a paper towel-lined plate to absorb excess oil.
8. Serve the Crispy Fried Perch with lemon wedges on the side.
9. Garnish with chopped fresh parsley.
10. Optionally, serve with tartar sauce for dipping.

SIDE DISHES

NOKEDLI (HUNGARIAN DUMPLINGS)

Servings: 4

Time: 20 minutes

Ingredients:

- 2 cups all-purpose flour
- 2 eggs
- 1/2 cup milk
- 1/2 tsp salt
- Water for boiling

Instructions:

1. In a mixing bowl, combine the flour and salt.

2. In a separate bowl, whisk together the eggs and milk.
3. Gradually add the wet ingredients to the dry ingredients, stirring continuously, until a thick batter forms.
4. Bring a large pot of salted water to a boil.
5. Spoon small portions of the batter into the boiling water. Use a spatula or the back of a spoon to push small bits of dough into the water.
6. Cook the dumplings for 2-3 minutes or until they float to the surface.
7. Using a slotted spoon, remove the dumplings from the water and drain.
8. Repeat the process until all the batter is used.
9. Serve the Nokedli as a side dish with your favorite Hungarian stews or sauces.

CUCUMBER SALAD (UBORKASALÁTA)

Servings: 4

Time: 15 minutes

Ingredients:

- 4 medium cucumbers, thinly sliced
- 1 small red onion, thinly sliced
- 1/4 cup chopped fresh dill
- 1/3 cup white vinegar
- 2 tbsp sugar
- 1/2 cup water
- Salt and pepper to taste
- Sour cream for garnish (optional)

Instructions:

1. In a large bowl, combine the sliced cucumbers, thinly sliced red onion, and chopped fresh dill.
2. In a separate bowl, whisk together white vinegar, sugar, water, salt, and pepper until the sugar is dissolved.
3. Pour the vinegar mixture over the cucumber mixture and toss well to coat.
4. Let the salad marinate in the refrigerator for at least 10 minutes to allow the flavors to meld.
5. Before serving, give the salad a good toss to ensure it's well coated with the dressing.
6. Optionally, garnish with a dollop of sour cream before serving.
7. Serve the refreshing Uborkasaláta as a delightful side dish to complement your Hungarian meal.

LECSO (HUNGARIAN EGGPLANT SPREAD)

Servings: 4

Time: 30 minutes

Ingredients:

- 2 large eggplants, diced
- 2 red bell peppers, diced
- 2 tomatoes, diced
- 1 onion, finely chopped
- 2 cloves garlic, minced
- 3 tbsp vegetable oil
- 1 tsp sweet paprika
- Salt and pepper to taste
- Chopped fresh parsley for garnish

Instructions:

1. In a large skillet, heat vegetable oil over medium heat.
2. Add finely chopped onions and minced garlic. Sauté until the onions are translucent.
3. Add diced eggplants, red bell peppers, and tomatoes to the skillet. Stir well to combine.
4. Sprinkle sweet paprika over the vegetables, ensuring even coverage.
5. Cook the mixture over medium heat, stirring occasionally, for about 20-25 minutes or until the vegetables are soft and well-cooked.
6. Season with salt and pepper to taste.
7. Garnish with chopped fresh parsley before serving.
8. Serve the Lecso as a flavorful spread or side dish, perfect for accompanying meats or bread.

STUFFED BELL PEPPERS WITH RICE (TÖLTÖTT PAPRIKA RIZZSEL)

Servings: 4

Time: 1.5 hours

Ingredients:

- 4 large bell peppers
- 1 cup rice, cooked
- 1 lb (450g) ground beef or pork
- 1 onion, finely chopped
- 2 cloves garlic, minced
- 2 tbsp vegetable oil
- 2 tbsp sweet paprika

- 1 tsp caraway seeds
- 1 cup tomato sauce
- Salt and pepper to taste
- Sour cream for serving
- Chopped fresh parsley for garnish

Instructions:

1. Preheat the oven to 375°F (190°C).
2. Cut the tops off the bell peppers and remove the seeds.
3. In a skillet, heat vegetable oil over medium heat. Add chopped onions and garlic. Sauté until the onions are translucent.
4. Add ground beef or pork to the skillet. Cook until browned, breaking it apart with a spoon.
5. Stir in cooked rice, sweet paprika, caraway seeds, salt, and pepper. Cook for a few minutes to blend the flavors.
6. Fill each bell pepper with the meat and rice mixture.
7. Place the stuffed peppers in a baking dish. Pour tomato sauce over the peppers.
8. Cover the baking dish with aluminum foil and bake for 45-50 minutes or until the peppers are tender.
9. Serve hot, topped with a dollop of sour cream and garnished with chopped fresh parsley.

BREADS

HUNGARIAN LÁNGOS BREAD

Servings: 4

Time: 2 hours (including rising time)

Ingredients:

For the Dough:

- 4 cups all-purpose flour
- 1 cup warm water
- 1 tsp sugar
- 1 packet (2 1/4 tsp) active dry yeast
- 1/2 cup milk, lukewarm
- 1 tsp salt

- Vegetable oil for frying

For Toppings:

- Garlic, minced
- Sour cream
- Grated cheese (optional)
- Chopped fresh parsley
- Salt

Instructions:

Preparing the Dough:

1. In a small bowl, combine warm water, sugar, and active dry yeast. Let it sit for 5-10 minutes until it becomes frothy.
2. In a large mixing bowl, combine the flour and salt.
3. Make a well in the center of the flour mixture and pour in the yeast mixture and lukewarm milk.
4. Gradually incorporate the flour into the wet ingredients until a dough forms.
5. Knead the dough on a floured surface for about 8-10 minutes until it becomes smooth and elastic.
6. Place the dough in a lightly oiled bowl, cover it with a clean kitchen towel, and let it rise in a warm place for 1 hour or until it doubles in size.

Making Lángos:

1. Punch down the risen dough and divide it into 4 equal portions.
2. On a floured surface, roll out each portion into a circle or oval shape, about 1/4 inch thick.

3. In a deep skillet or frying pan, heat vegetable oil over medium-high heat.
4. Carefully place a portion of the rolled-out dough into the hot oil and fry until it becomes golden brown on both sides (about 2-3 minutes per side).
5. Remove the lángos from the oil and place it on paper towels to absorb excess oil.

Toppings:

1. While the lángos is still hot, rub the surface with minced garlic.
2. Spread sour cream over the top, and if desired, sprinkle with grated cheese, chopped fresh parsley, and a pinch of salt.
3. Repeat the process for the remaining portions of dough.
4. Serve the Hungarian Lángos Bread warm and enjoy this delicious, crispy treat!

Lángos is a versatile bread, and you can experiment with various toppings like shredded cabbage, sausages, or even Nutella for a sweet version.

WALNUT ROLL (DIÓS BEIGLI)

Servings: 12 slices

Time: 3 hours (including rising and baking time)

Ingredients:

For the Dough:

- 4 cups all-purpose flour
- 1 cup unsalted butter, softened
- 1/2 cup granulated sugar
- 3 egg yolks
- 1 cup milk, lukewarm
- 1 packet (2 1/4 tsp) active dry yeast
- Pinch of salt

For the Filling:

- 2 cups ground walnuts
- 1 cup granulated sugar
- 1 cup milk
- 1 tsp vanilla extract

For Assembly:

- 1 egg, beaten (for egg wash)
- Powdered sugar for dusting

Instructions:

Preparing the Dough:

1. In a small bowl, combine lukewarm milk and active dry yeast. Let it sit for 5-10 minutes until it becomes frothy.
2. In a large mixing bowl, cream together the softened butter and sugar until light and fluffy.
3. Add the egg yolks one at a time, beating well after each addition.
4. Pour in the yeast mixture and mix until combined.
5. Gradually add the flour and a pinch of salt, kneading the dough until it becomes smooth.

6. Divide the dough into two equal portions, shape them into balls, and place them in lightly oiled bowls. Cover and let them rise in a warm place for 1-2 hours or until doubled in size.

Preparing the Filling:

1. In a saucepan, combine ground walnuts, sugar, and milk.
2. Cook over medium heat, stirring constantly, until the mixture thickens.
3. Remove from heat, stir in vanilla extract, and let the filling cool.

Assembling the Walnut Roll:

1. Preheat the oven to 350°F (175°C).
2. Roll out one portion of the dough on a floured surface into a rectangle.
3. Spread half of the walnut filling evenly over the rolled-out dough.
4. Roll the dough tightly from one of the longer sides, forming a log.
5. Repeat the process with the second portion of the dough.
6. Place both rolls on a parchment-lined baking sheet.
7. Brush the tops of the rolls with beaten egg for a golden finish.
8. Bake in the preheated oven for 25-30 minutes or until the tops are golden brown.
9. Allow the Walnut Rolls to cool before slicing.
10. Dust with powdered sugar before serving.

POPPY SEED ROLL (MÁKOS BEIGLI)

Servings: 12 slices

Time: 3 hours (including rising and baking time)

Ingredients:

For the Dough:

- 4 cups all-purpose flour
- 1 cup unsalted butter, softened
- 1/2 cup granulated sugar
- 3 egg yolks
- 1 cup milk, lukewarm
- 1 packet (2 1/4 tsp) active dry yeast
- Pinch of salt

For the Filling:

- 2 cups poppy seeds, ground
- 1 cup milk
- 1 cup granulated sugar
- 1 tsp vanilla extract

For Assembly:

- 1 egg, beaten (for egg wash)
- Powdered sugar for dusting

Instructions:

Preparing the Dough:

1. In a small bowl, combine lukewarm milk and active dry yeast. Let it sit for 5-10 minutes until it becomes frothy.

2. In a large mixing bowl, cream together the softened butter and sugar until light and fluffy.
3. Add the egg yolks one at a time, beating well after each addition.
4. Pour in the yeast mixture and mix until combined.
5. Gradually add the flour and a pinch of salt, kneading the dough until it becomes smooth.
6. Divide the dough into two equal portions, shape them into balls, and place them in lightly oiled bowls. Cover and let them rise in a warm place for 1-2 hours or until doubled in size.

Preparing the Filling:

1. In a saucepan, combine ground poppy seeds, sugar, and milk.
2. Cook over medium heat, stirring constantly, until the mixture thickens.
3. Remove from heat, stir in vanilla extract, and let the filling cool.

Assembling the Poppy Seed Roll:

1. Preheat the oven to 350°F (175°C).
2. Roll out one portion of the dough on a floured surface into a rectangle.
3. Spread half of the poppy seed filling evenly over the rolled-out dough.
4. Roll the dough tightly from one of the longer sides, forming a log.
5. Repeat the process with the second portion of the dough.
6. Place both rolls on a parchment-lined baking sheet.

7. Brush the tops of the rolls with beaten egg for a golden finish.
8. Bake in the preheated oven for 25-30 minutes or until the tops are golden brown.
9. Allow the Poppy Seed Rolls to cool before slicing.
10. Dust with powdered sugar before serving.

HUNGARIAN CRESCENT ROLLS (KIFLI)

Servings: 24 rolls

Time: 2.5 hours (including rising and baking time)

Ingredients:

For the Dough:

- 4 cups all-purpose flour
- 1 cup unsalted butter, softened
- 1/2 cup sour cream
- 2 egg yolks
- 1 packet (2 1/4 tsp) active dry yeast
- 1/4 cup warm water
- 1/4 cup granulated sugar
- 1/2 tsp salt

For the Filling:

- Apricot or plum jam (or filling of your choice)

For Assembly:

- Powdered sugar for dusting

Instructions:

Preparing the Dough:

1. In a small bowl, combine warm water, sugar, and active dry yeast. Let it sit for 5-10 minutes until it becomes frothy.
2. In a large mixing bowl, cream together the softened butter, sour cream, and egg yolks.
3. Add the yeast mixture to the creamed ingredients and mix until well combined.
4. Gradually add the flour and salt, kneading the dough until it becomes smooth.
5. Divide the dough into four equal portions, shape them into balls, and place them in lightly oiled bowls. Cover and let them rise in a warm place for 1-2 hours or until doubled in size.

Assembling the Crescent Rolls:

1. Preheat the oven to 350°F (175°C).
2. On a floured surface, roll out one portion of the dough into a circle.
3. Spread a thin layer of apricot or plum jam over the rolled-out dough.
4. Cut the circle into 6 wedges.
5. Starting from the wide end, roll each wedge towards the point, forming a crescent shape.
6. Place the crescent rolls on a parchment-lined baking sheet.
7. Repeat the process with the remaining portions of dough.
8. Bake in the preheated oven for 15-20 minutes or until the tops are golden brown.

9. Allow the Hungarian Crescent Rolls (Kifli) to cool before dusting with powdered sugar.
10. Serve these delightful, flaky rolls as a sweet treat for any occasion.

POTATO BREAD (KRUMPLIS KENYÉR)

Servings: 1 loaf

Time: 3 hours (including rising and baking time)

Ingredients:

- 1 cup mashed potatoes (cooled)
- 1 cup warm milk
- 1 packet (2 1/4 tsp) active dry yeast
- 1/4 cup warm water
- 2 tbsp honey or sugar
- 4 cups all-purpose flour
- 1/4 cup unsalted butter, melted
- 1 tsp salt

Instructions:

1. In a small bowl, combine warm water, honey (or sugar), and active dry yeast. Let it sit for 5-10 minutes until it becomes frothy.
2. In a large mixing bowl, combine mashed potatoes and warm milk.
3. Add the yeast mixture to the potato and milk mixture. Mix well.
4. Gradually add the flour and salt, kneading the dough until it becomes smooth.

5. Incorporate the melted butter into the dough, ensuring it's evenly distributed.
6. Place the dough in a lightly oiled bowl, cover it with a clean kitchen towel, and let it rise in a warm place for 1-2 hours or until it doubles in size.
7. Preheat the oven to 375°F (190°C).
8. Punch down the risen dough and shape it into a loaf.
9. Place the shaped dough in a greased loaf pan.
10. Cover the pan with a clean kitchen towel and let the dough rise for an additional 30-45 minutes.
11. Bake in the preheated oven for 30-35 minutes or until the top is golden brown and the bread sounds hollow when tapped.
12. Allow the Potato Bread (Krumplis Kenyér) to cool before slicing.
13. Serve as a versatile accompaniment to meals or enjoy it toasted with your favorite spreads.

VEGETARIAN DELIGHTS

LENTIL AND VEGETABLE STEW

Servings: 6

Time: 1.5 hours

Ingredients:

- 1 cup dry lentils, rinsed and drained
- 2 tbsp olive oil
- 1 onion, finely chopped
- 2 carrots, diced
- 2 celery stalks, diced
- 3 cloves garlic, minced
- 1 bell pepper, diced
- 1 zucchini, diced

- 1 can (14 oz) diced tomatoes
- 4 cups vegetable broth
- 1 tsp paprika
- 1 tsp cumin
- 1/2 tsp thyme
- Salt and pepper to taste
- Fresh parsley for garnish

Instructions:

1. In a large pot, heat olive oil over medium heat.
2. Add chopped onions and sauté until they become translucent.
3. Stir in minced garlic and cook for an additional 1-2 minutes.
4. Add diced carrots, celery, bell pepper, and zucchini to the pot. Sauté the vegetables until they start to soften.
5. Pour in vegetable broth and add dry lentils, diced tomatoes, paprika, cumin, thyme, salt, and pepper. Stir well to combine.
6. Bring the stew to a boil, then reduce the heat to low, cover, and simmer for 45-60 minutes or until the lentils are tender.
7. Adjust the seasoning if needed.
8. Serve the Lentil and Vegetable Stew hot, garnished with fresh parsley.

MUSHROOM PAPRIKASH

Servings: 4

Time: 30 minutes

Ingredients:

- 1 lb (450g) mushrooms, sliced
- 2 tbsp olive oil
- 1 onion, finely chopped
- 2 cloves garlic, minced
- 2 tbsp sweet paprika
- 1 cup vegetable broth
- 1 cup sour cream
- Salt and pepper to taste
- Chopped fresh parsley for garnish
- Cooked egg noodles or rice for serving

Instructions:

1. In a large skillet, heat olive oil over medium heat.
2. Add chopped onions and sauté until they become translucent.
3. Stir in minced garlic and cook for an additional 1-2 minutes.
4. Add sliced mushrooms to the skillet and cook until they release their moisture and become tender.
5. Sprinkle sweet paprika over the mushrooms, ensuring even coverage.
6. Pour in vegetable broth and bring the mixture to a simmer.
7. Reduce the heat to low and stir in sour cream. Simmer for an additional 5-7 minutes, allowing the flavors to meld.
8. Season with salt and pepper to taste.
9. Serve the Mushroom Paprikash over cooked egg noodles or rice.
10. Garnish with chopped fresh parsley.

EGGPLANT PAPRIKASH

Servings: 4

Time: 45 minutes

Ingredients:

- 2 large eggplants, diced
- 3 tbsp olive oil
- 1 onion, finely chopped
- 2 cloves garlic, minced
- 2 tbsp sweet paprika
- 1 can (14 oz) diced tomatoes
- 1 cup vegetable broth
- Salt and pepper to taste
- 1/2 cup sour cream
- Chopped fresh parsley for garnish
- Cooked rice or pasta for serving

Instructions:

1. In a large skillet, heat olive oil over medium heat.
2. Add chopped onions and sauté until they become translucent.
3. Stir in minced garlic and cook for an additional 1-2 minutes.
4. Add diced eggplants to the skillet and cook until they are softened and lightly browned.
5. Sprinkle sweet paprika over the eggplants, ensuring even coverage.
6. Pour in diced tomatoes and vegetable broth. Stir well to combine.

7. Season with salt and pepper to taste. Bring the mixture to a simmer.
8. Reduce the heat to low, cover the skillet, and let it simmer for 20-25 minutes or until the eggplants are fully cooked.
9. Stir in sour cream, ensuring it's well incorporated into the sauce.
10. Adjust the seasoning if needed.
11. Serve the Eggplant Paprikash over cooked rice or pasta.
12. Garnish with chopped fresh parsley.

CABBAGE AND NOODLES (KAPOSZTÁS TÉSZTA)

Servings: 4

Time: 30 minutes

Ingredients:

- 8 oz (225g) egg noodles
- 3 tbsp vegetable oil
- 1 onion, finely chopped
- 4 cups shredded cabbage
- 1 tsp sweet paprika
- Salt and pepper to taste
- Chopped fresh parsley for garnish

Instructions:

1. Cook the egg noodles according to the package instructions. Drain and set aside.
2. In a large skillet, heat vegetable oil over medium heat.

3. Add chopped onions and sauté until they become translucent.
4. Stir in shredded cabbage and cook until it wilts and becomes tender.
5. Sprinkle sweet paprika over the cabbage, ensuring even coverage.
6. Add the cooked egg noodles to the skillet and toss well to combine with the cabbage.
7. Season with salt and pepper to taste. Stir to incorporate the flavors.
8. Cook for an additional 5-7 minutes, allowing the noodles to absorb the flavors of the cabbage.
9. Adjust the seasoning if needed.
10. Serve the Cabbage and Noodles hot, garnished with chopped fresh parsley.

PASTA AND DUMPLINGS

HUNGARIAN NOODLES WITH CABBAGE (KÁPOSZTÁS TÉSZTA)

Servings: 4

Time: 30 minutes

Ingredients:

- 8 oz (225g) egg noodles
- 3 tbsp vegetable oil
- 1 onion, finely chopped
- 4 cups shredded cabbage
- 1 tsp sweet paprika
- Salt and pepper to taste
- Chopped fresh parsley for garnish

Instructions:

1. Cook the egg noodles according to the package instructions. Drain and set aside.
2. In a large skillet, heat vegetable oil over medium heat.
3. Add chopped onions and sauté until they become translucent.
4. Stir in shredded cabbage and cook until it wilts and becomes tender.
5. Sprinkle sweet paprika over the cabbage, ensuring even coverage.
6. Add the cooked egg noodles to the skillet and toss well to combine with the cabbage.
7. Season with salt and pepper to taste. Stir to incorporate the flavors.
8. Cook for an additional 5-7 minutes, allowing the noodles to absorb the flavors of the cabbage.
9. Adjust the seasoning if needed.
10. Serve the Hungarian Noodles with Cabbage hot, garnished with chopped fresh parsley.

COTTAGE CHEESE NOODLES (TÚRÓS CSUSZA)

Servings: 4

Time: 25 minutes

Ingredients:

- 8 oz (225g) egg noodles
- 2 tbsp butter
- 1 onion, finely chopped

- 1 cup cottage cheese
- 1/2 cup sour cream
- Salt and black pepper to taste
- Chopped fresh chives for garnish

Instructions:

1. Cook the egg noodles according to the package instructions. Drain and set aside.
2. In a large skillet, melt butter over medium heat.
3. Add chopped onions and sauté until they become translucent.
4. Reduce the heat to low, then stir in cottage cheese and sour cream. Mix well until the cottage cheese is melted and combined with the sour cream.
5. Add the cooked egg noodles to the skillet and toss gently to coat them with the cottage cheese mixture.
6. Season with salt and black pepper to taste. Stir to incorporate the flavors.
7. Cook for an additional 3-5 minutes, allowing the noodles to absorb the creamy mixture.
8. Adjust the seasoning if needed.
9. Serve the Cottage Cheese Noodles (Túrós Csusza) hot, garnished with chopped fresh chives.

PLUM DUMPLINGS (SZILVÁS GOMBÓC)

Servings: 4-6

Time: 1.5 hours

Ingredients:

For the Dough:

- 2 cups mashed potatoes, cooled
- 2 cups all-purpose flour
- 1/2 tsp salt
- 1 egg

For the Filling:

- 12 small plums, pitted
- 1/2 cup granulated sugar
- 1 tsp ground cinnamon

For Topping:

- 1 cup breadcrumbs
- 4 tbsp unsalted butter, melted
- 2 tbsp granulated sugar
- Ground cinnamon for sprinkling

Instructions:

Preparing the Dough:

1. In a large bowl, combine mashed potatoes, all-purpose flour, salt, and egg. Knead the mixture until it forms a smooth dough.
2. Divide the dough into golf ball-sized portions.

Preparing the Filling:

1. Mix together granulated sugar and ground cinnamon in a small bowl.

2. Take each pitted plum and stuff it with a small amount of the sugar-cinnamon mixture.

Assembling the Dumplings:

1. Take one portion of the dough and flatten it into a small disc.
2. Place a stuffed plum in the center of the disc and wrap the dough around it, forming a smooth ball.
3. Repeat the process for the remaining plums.

Cooking the Dumplings:

1. Bring a large pot of salted water to a boil.
2. Carefully place the plum dumplings into the boiling water. Cook in batches, ensuring not to overcrowd the pot.
3. Boil the dumplings for 10-12 minutes or until they float to the surface.
4. Using a slotted spoon, remove the dumplings and let them drain briefly.

Preparing the Topping:

1. In a skillet, toast the breadcrumbs over medium heat until golden brown.
2. Drizzle melted butter over the toasted breadcrumbs and stir to coat.

Final Assembly:

1. Roll each boiled plum dumpling in the buttered breadcrumbs until fully coated.

2. Sprinkle granulated sugar and ground cinnamon over the top.
3. Serve the Plum Dumplings (Szilvás Gombóc) warm.

CHERRY DUMPLINGS (MEGGYES GOMBÓC)

Servings: 4-6

Time: 1.5 hours

Ingredients:

For the Dough:

- 2 cups mashed potatoes, cooled
- 2 cups all-purpose flour
- 1/2 tsp salt
- 1 egg

For the Filling:

- 1 cup fresh or canned cherries, pitted
- 1/4 cup granulated sugar
- 1/2 tsp vanilla extract

For Topping:

- 1 cup breadcrumbs
- 4 tbsp unsalted butter, melted
- 2 tbsp powdered sugar
- Ground cinnamon for sprinkling

Instructions:

Preparing the Dough:

1. In a large bowl, combine mashed potatoes, all-purpose flour, salt, and egg. Knead the mixture until it forms a smooth dough.
2. Divide the dough into golf ball-sized portions.

Preparing the Filling:

1. Mix together pitted cherries, granulated sugar, and vanilla extract in a bowl. Set aside.

Assembling the Dumplings:

1. Take one portion of the dough and flatten it into a small disc.
2. Place a spoonful of the cherry filling in the center of the disc and wrap the dough around it, forming a smooth ball.
3. Repeat the process for the remaining cherries.

Cooking the Dumplings:

1. Bring a large pot of salted water to a boil.
2. Carefully place the cherry dumplings into the boiling water. Cook in batches, ensuring not to overcrowd the pot.
3. Boil the dumplings for 10-12 minutes or until they float to the surface.
4. Using a slotted spoon, remove the dumplings and let them drain briefly.

Preparing the Topping:

1. In a skillet, toast the breadcrumbs over medium heat until golden brown.
2. Drizzle melted butter over the toasted breadcrumbs and stir to coat.

Final Assembly:

1. Roll each boiled cherry dumpling in the buttered breadcrumbs until fully coated.
2. Sprinkle powdered sugar and ground cinnamon over the top.
3. Serve the Cherry Dumplings (Meggyes Gombóc) warm.

DESSERTS

DOBOS TORTE

Servings: 12

Time: 2 hours

Ingredients:

For the Cake Layers:

- 6 large eggs, separated
- 1 cup granulated sugar
- 1 cup all-purpose flour
- 1 tsp baking powder
- 1/2 cup unsalted butter, melted and cooled
- 1 tsp vanilla extract

For the Chocolate Buttercream:

- 1 cup unsalted butter, softened
- 2 cups powdered sugar
- 200g dark chocolate, melted and cooled
- 1 tsp vanilla extract

For the Caramel Topping:

- 1 cup granulated sugar
- 1/4 cup water

Instructions:

Preparing the Cake Layers:

1. Preheat the oven to 350°F (175°C). Grease and flour six 9-inch cake pans.
2. In a large bowl, beat egg yolks with sugar until light and fluffy.
3. In a separate bowl, sift together flour and baking powder.
4. Gradually add the dry ingredients to the egg yolk mixture, mixing well.
5. Stir in melted butter and vanilla extract.
6. In another clean, dry bowl, beat egg whites until stiff peaks form.
7. Gently fold the egg whites into the batter until well combined.
8. Divide the batter evenly among the prepared cake pans and smooth the tops.
9. Bake for 10-12 minutes or until a toothpick inserted into the center comes out clean.
10. Allow the cake layers to cool completely.

Preparing the Chocolate Buttercream:

1. In a mixing bowl, beat softened butter until creamy.
2. Gradually add powdered sugar, melted chocolate, and vanilla extract. Beat until smooth and well combined.
3. Refrigerate the chocolate buttercream until it thickens slightly.

Assembling the Dobos Torte:

1. Place one cake layer on a serving plate and spread a thin layer of chocolate buttercream over it.
2. Repeat the process, stacking the cake layers with chocolate buttercream between each.
3. Use the remaining chocolate buttercream to frost the top and sides of the assembled cake.

Preparing the Caramel Topping:

1. In a saucepan, combine granulated sugar and water. Cook over medium heat, swirling the pan occasionally, until the sugar turns into a golden caramel color.
2. Remove from heat and drizzle the caramel over the frosted cake, spreading it quickly with a spatula.
3. Allow the caramel to set before slicing and serving.

HUNGARIAN APPLE STRUDEL (ALMÁS RÉTES)

Servings: 8-10

Time: 1.5 hours

Ingredients:

For the Dough:

- 2 cups all-purpose flour
- 1/4 cup vegetable oil
- 1/2 cup warm water
- 1/2 tsp salt
- 1 large egg

For the Filling:

- 6 cups apples, peeled, cored, and thinly sliced
- 1 cup granulated sugar
- 1 cup breadcrumbs
- 1 tsp ground cinnamon
- 1/2 cup raisins (optional)
- Zest of 1 lemon

For Assembly:

- 1/2 cup unsalted butter, melted
- Powdered sugar for dusting

Instructions:

Preparing the Dough:

1. In a large bowl, combine flour and salt. Make a well in the center.
2. In a separate bowl, whisk together warm water, vegetable oil, and egg.

3. Pour the wet ingredients into the well of the flour mixture. Knead the dough until it becomes smooth and elastic.
4. Form the dough into a ball, coat it lightly with oil, cover, and let it rest for 30 minutes.

Preparing the Filling:

1. In a bowl, combine sliced apples, granulated sugar, breadcrumbs, ground cinnamon, raisins (if using), and lemon zest. Mix well.

Assembling the Strudel:

1. Preheat the oven to 350°F (175°C). Line a baking sheet with parchment paper.
2. On a floured surface, roll out the dough into a large rectangle, thin enough to see through.
3. Brush the rolled-out dough with melted butter.
4. Evenly spread the apple filling over the dough, leaving a border around the edges.
5. Fold in the sides of the dough and roll it up tightly, sealing the edges.
6. Transfer the strudel to the prepared baking sheet.
7. Brush the top of the strudel with additional melted butter.

Baking the Strudel:

1. Bake in the preheated oven for 45-50 minutes or until the strudel is golden brown.
2. Remove from the oven and let it cool slightly before dusting with powdered sugar.
3. Slice and serve the Hungarian Apple Strudel warm.

SOMLÓI GALUSKA

Servings: 8-10

Time: 2 hours

Ingredients:

For the Pancakes:

- 3 large eggs
- 1 cup milk
- 1 cup all-purpose flour
- 1/4 cup unsalted butter, melted
- 1/4 cup granulated sugar
- 1 tsp vanilla extract
- 1/2 tsp baking powder
- Pinch of salt

For the Chocolate Sauce:

- 1 cup dark chocolate, chopped
- 1 cup heavy cream
- 2 tbsp granulated sugar

For the Walnut Filling:

- 1 cup walnuts, finely chopped
- 1/4 cup granulated sugar
- 1 cup heavy cream, whipped

For Assembly:

- 1 cup rum (for soaking the pancakes)

- Whipped cream for garnish
- Grated chocolate for garnish

Instructions:

Preparing the Pancakes:

1. In a bowl, whisk together eggs, milk, melted butter, sugar, and vanilla extract.
2. In another bowl, sift together flour, baking powder, and a pinch of salt.
3. Gradually add the dry ingredients to the wet ingredients, mixing until a smooth batter forms.
4. Heat a non-stick skillet over medium heat. Pour a small amount of batter onto the skillet to make thin pancakes. Cook each side until golden brown.
5. Repeat until all the batter is used, stacking the pancakes on a plate.

Preparing the Chocolate Sauce:

1. In a saucepan, heat heavy cream until it begins to simmer.
2. Remove from heat and add chopped dark chocolate and sugar. Stir until the chocolate is fully melted and the sauce is smooth.

Preparing the Walnut Filling:

1. In a bowl, mix together finely chopped walnuts and sugar.
2. Gently fold in whipped cream until well combined.

Assembling Somlói Galuska:

1. Soak each pancake in rum briefly.
2. On a serving platter, layer the soaked pancakes with the walnut filling between each layer.
3. Pour the warm chocolate sauce over the assembled pancakes.
4. Garnish with additional whipped cream and grated chocolate.
5. Allow the Somlói Galuska to set for at least 1 hour before serving.

RÁKÓCZI TÚRÓS

Servings: 8-10

Time: 1.5 hours

Ingredients:

For the Dough:

- 2 cups all-purpose flour
- 1/2 cup unsalted butter, cold and diced
- 1/4 cup granulated sugar
- 1/2 cup sour cream
- 1 tsp baking powder
- Pinch of salt

For the Cottage Cheese Filling:

- 3 cups cottage cheese
- 1/2 cup granulated sugar
- 1 tsp vanilla extract
- 3 large eggs

- 1/4 cup raisins (optional)

For Assembly:

- 1/4 cup apricot jam
- Powdered sugar for dusting

Instructions:

Preparing the Dough:

1. In a food processor, combine flour, cold diced butter, sugar, sour cream, baking powder, and a pinch of salt. Pulse until the mixture resembles coarse crumbs.
2. Turn the mixture onto a floured surface and knead it into a smooth dough.
3. Wrap the dough in plastic wrap and refrigerate for at least 30 minutes.

Preparing the Cottage Cheese Filling:

1. In a bowl, mix together cottage cheese, granulated sugar, vanilla extract, eggs, and raisins (if using).
2. Set aside the cottage cheese filling.

Assembling Rákóczi Túrós:

1. Preheat the oven to 350°F (175°C). Grease a 9-inch springform pan.
2. Roll out two-thirds of the chilled dough and line the bottom and sides of the prepared pan.
3. Spread the cottage cheese filling over the dough.

4. Roll out the remaining dough and cut it into strips. Arrange the strips in a lattice pattern over the cottage cheese filling.
5. Bake in the preheated oven for 45-50 minutes or until the crust is golden brown.

Final Touch:

1. Warm apricot jam in a small saucepan until it becomes liquid.
2. Brush the warm apricot jam over the lattice crust.
3. Allow the Rákóczi Túrós to cool before dusting with powdered sugar.
4. Slice and serve this delightful Hungarian dessert, a perfect blend of sweet cottage cheese filling and tender crust!

ESTERHÁZY TORTE

Servings: 12

Time: 3 hours

Ingredients:

For the Sponge Cake:

- 6 large eggs, separated
- 1 cup granulated sugar
- 1 cup ground almonds
- 1/2 cup all-purpose flour
- 1 tsp baking powder
- 1/2 cup unsalted butter, melted and cooled

- 1 tsp vanilla extract

For the Walnut Filling:

- 2 cups ground walnuts
- 1 cup powdered sugar
- 1/2 cup milk
- 1 tsp vanilla extract
- 1/2 cup unsalted butter, softened

For the Icing:

- 1 1/2 cups powdered sugar
- 2 tbsp cocoa powder
- 2 tbsp milk
- 1 tsp instant coffee

Instructions:

Preparing the Sponge Cake:

1. Preheat the oven to 350°F (175°C). Grease and flour three 9-inch cake pans.
2. In a large bowl, beat egg yolks with sugar until light and fluffy.
3. In a separate bowl, sift together ground almonds, flour, and baking powder.
4. Gradually add the dry ingredients to the egg yolk mixture, mixing well.
5. Stir in melted butter and vanilla extract.
6. In another clean, dry bowl, beat egg whites until stiff peaks form.
7. Gently fold the egg whites into the batter until well combined.

8. Divide the batter evenly among the prepared cake pans and smooth the tops.
9. Bake for 15-18 minutes or until a toothpick inserted into the center comes out clean.
10. Allow the cake layers to cool completely.

Preparing the Walnut Filling:

1. In a bowl, combine ground walnuts, powdered sugar, milk, vanilla extract, and softened butter. Mix until well combined.

Assembling Esterházy Torte:

1. Place one cake layer on a serving plate and spread a generous layer of the walnut filling over it.
2. Repeat the process, stacking the cake layers with walnut filling between each.
3. Use the remaining walnut filling to frost the top and sides of the assembled cake.

Preparing the Icing:

1. In a bowl, whisk together powdered sugar, cocoa powder, milk, and instant coffee until smooth.
2. Drizzle the icing over the top of the cake, allowing it to drip down the sides.
3. Chill the Esterházy Torte in the refrigerator for at least 2 hours before serving.

CHESTNUT PUREE (GESZTENYEPÜRÉ)

Servings: 4-6

Time: 45 minutes

Ingredients:

- 2 cups fresh chestnuts
- 1 cup milk
- 1/2 cup granulated sugar
- 1 tsp vanilla extract
- Pinch of salt
- 1/2 cup heavy cream, whipped (for serving)
- Ground cinnamon for garnish

Instructions:

Preparing the Chestnuts:

1. Preheat the oven to 400°F (200°C).
2. Using a sharp knife, make a small incision on the flat side of each chestnut.
3. Place the chestnuts on a baking sheet and roast in the preheated oven for 20-25 minutes or until the skins begin to peel away.
4. Remove the chestnuts from the oven and let them cool slightly.
5. Peel the outer shell and inner skin from the chestnuts. This is easier to do while they are still warm.

Making the Chestnut Puree:

1. In a saucepan, combine peeled chestnuts, milk, sugar, vanilla extract, and a pinch of salt.
2. Bring the mixture to a simmer over medium heat.
3. Reduce the heat to low and let it simmer gently for 15-20 minutes or until the chestnuts are tender.

4. Remove from heat and allow the mixture to cool slightly.
5. Using a blender or food processor, puree the chestnut mixture until smooth and creamy.
6. If the puree is too thick, you can add more milk to achieve the desired consistency.

Serving:

1. Spoon the Chestnut Puree into serving dishes.
2. Top with a dollop of whipped cream.
3. Sprinkle ground cinnamon over the whipped cream for garnish.
4. Serve the Gesztenyepüré warm or chilled.

GERBEAUD SLICE (ZSERBÓ)

Servings: 12

Time: 2 hours

Ingredients:

For the Dough:

- 2 cups all-purpose flour
- 1/2 cup granulated sugar
- 1 cup unsalted butter, cold and diced
- 2 large egg yolks
- 1/4 cup sour cream

For the Walnut Filling:

- 2 cups ground walnuts

- 1 cup powdered sugar
- 1/2 cup unsalted butter, melted
- 1 tsp vanilla extract
- 1/4 cup apricot jam

For the Chocolate Glaze:

- 4 oz (115g) dark chocolate, chopped
- 1/2 cup unsalted butter

Instructions:

Preparing the Dough:

1. In a large bowl, combine flour and sugar.
2. Add cold, diced butter and mix until the mixture resembles coarse crumbs.
3. Stir in egg yolks and sour cream. Mix until the dough comes together.
4. Divide the dough into two equal portions, shape them into rectangles, wrap in plastic wrap, and refrigerate for at least 30 minutes.

Preparing the Walnut Filling:

1. In a bowl, combine ground walnuts, powdered sugar, melted butter, and vanilla extract. Mix until well combined.
2. Preheat the oven to 350°F (175°C).
3. Roll out one portion of the chilled dough and press it into the bottom of a 9x13-inch baking pan lined with parchment paper.
4. Spread the apricot jam over the rolled-out dough.
5. Evenly distribute the walnut filling over the apricot jam.

6. Roll out the second portion of the chilled dough and place it over the walnut filling, pressing the edges to seal.
7. Bake in the preheated oven for 30-35 minutes or until the top is golden brown.

Preparing the Chocolate Glaze:

1. In a heatproof bowl, melt dark chocolate and butter over a double boiler or in the microwave.
2. Stir until smooth and well combined.

Final Touch:

1. Allow the Gerbeaud Slice (Zserbó) to cool in the pan for about 15 minutes.
2. Pour the chocolate glaze over the top, spreading it evenly.
3. Let the slice cool completely before cutting it into squares.

RÁKÓCZI TÚRÓS

Servings: 8-10

Time: 1.5 hours

Ingredients:

For the Dough:

- 2 cups all-purpose flour
- 1/2 cup unsalted butter, cold and diced
- 1/4 cup granulated sugar

- 1/2 cup sour cream
- 1 tsp baking powder
- Pinch of salt

For the Cottage Cheese Filling:

- 3 cups cottage cheese
- 1/2 cup granulated sugar
- 1 tsp vanilla extract
- 3 large eggs
- 1/4 cup raisins (optional)

For Assembly:

- 1/4 cup apricot jam
- Powdered sugar for dusting

Instructions:

Preparing the Dough:

1. In a large bowl, combine flour and sugar.
2. Add cold, diced butter and mix until the mixture resembles coarse crumbs.
3. Stir in sour cream, baking powder, and a pinch of salt. Mix until the dough comes together.
4. Divide the dough into two equal portions, shape them into rectangles, wrap in plastic wrap, and refrigerate for at least 30 minutes.

Preparing the Cottage Cheese Filling:

1. In a bowl, mix together cottage cheese, granulated sugar, vanilla extract, eggs, and raisins (if using).

2. Set aside the cottage cheese filling.

Assembling Rákóczi Túrós:

1. Preheat the oven to 350°F (175°C). Grease a 9-inch springform pan.
2. Roll out one portion of the chilled dough and press it into the bottom of the prepared pan.
3. Spread the apricot jam over the rolled-out dough.
4. Evenly distribute the cottage cheese filling over the apricot jam.
5. Roll out the second portion of the chilled dough and place it over the cottage cheese filling, pressing the edges to seal.
6. Bake in the preheated oven for 40-45 minutes or until the top is golden brown.

Final Touch:

1. Allow the Rákóczi Túrós to cool in the pan for about 15 minutes.
2. Dust the top with powdered sugar.
3. Slice and serve.

MEASUREMENT CONVERSIONS

Volume Conversions:

- 1 cup = 8 fluid ounces = 240 milliliters
- 1 tablespoon = 3 teaspoons = 15 milliliters
- 1 fluid ounce = 2 tablespoons = 30 milliliters
- 1 quart = 4 cups = 32 fluid ounces = 946 milliliters
- 1 gallon = 4 quarts = 128 fluid ounces = 3.78 liters
- 1 liter = 1,000 milliliters = 33.8 fluid ounces
- 1 milliliter = 0.034 fluid ounces = 0.002 cups

Weight Conversions:

- 1 pound = 16 ounces = 453.592 grams
- 1 ounce = 28.349 grams
- 1 gram = 0.035 ounces = 0.001 kilograms
- 1 kilogram = 1,000 grams = 35.274 ounces = 2.205 pounds

Temperature Conversions:

- To convert from Fahrenheit to Celsius: (°F - 32) / 1.8
- To convert from Celsius to Fahrenheit: (°C * 1.8) + 32

Length Conversions:

- 1 inch = 2.54 centimeters
- 1 foot = 12 inches = 30.48 centimeters
- 1 yard = 3 feet = 36 inches = 91.44 centimeters
- 1 meter = 100 centimeters = 1.094 yards
- 1 kilometer = 1,000 meters = 0.621 miles.

Printed in Great Britain
by Amazon